Little Science Stories

Test It

T0014535

By Amanda Gebhardt

2 Did you make this
brand new tool?

Does it work?
How will you know?

4 Make a test. Follow steps.

Ask if it will work this way.

6 Plan the test. Set it up.

Test it. Write up the result.

Switch it up. Will it
work that way?

Plan the test. Set it up.

Test it. Write up the result.

One last time. Switch it up.

Did it work this time?
Write that up, too.

Think and think. What did
each test show?

Word List

science words

Plan   Test
result   tool
steps   work
test

sight words

a   result
Does   the
Follow   What
How   work
One

Vowel Teams

/ā/ay	/ē/ea	/ō/ow	/o͞o/ew, oo, ou
way	each	know	new
		show	too
			tool
			you

Try It!

Make a tool and test it. Lay a pen down. Set a ruler across it. Place an object on one end of the ruler. Press the other side to lift the object. Did it work? Try a bigger object. Test it again!

81 Words

Did you make this brand new tool?

Does it work? How will you know?

Make a test. Follow steps.

Ask if it will work this way.

Plan the test. Set it up.

Test it. Write up the result.

Switch it up. Will it work that way?

Plan the test. Set it up.

Test it. Write up the result.

One last time. Switch it up.

Did it work this time? Write that up, too.

Think and think. What did each test show?

Published in the United States of America by Cherry Lake Publishing Group
Ann Arbor, Michigan
www.cherrylakepublishing.com

Photo Credits: © FAMILY STOCK/Shutterstock, cover, title page; © FAMILY STOCK/Shutterstock, 2–13; © Johnny Dao/Shutterstock, back cover

Cherry Blossom Press is an imprint of Cherry Lake Publishing Group.

Library of Congress Cataloging-in-Publication Data

Names: Gebhardt, Amanda, author.
Title: Test it / written by Amanda Gebhardt.
Description: Ann Arbor, Michigan : Cherry Blossom Press, [2024] | Series:
    Little science stories | Audience: Grades K-1 | Summary: "Learn about
    scientific processes in this decodable science book for beginning
    readers. A combination of domain-specific sight words and sequenced
    phonics skills builds confidence in content area reading. Bold, colorful
    photographs align directly with the text to help readers strengthen
    comprehension"– Provided by publisher.
Identifiers: LCCN 2023035059 | ISBN 9781668937686 (paperback) | ISBN
    9781668940068 (ebook) | ISBN 9781668941416 (pdf)
Subjects: LCSH: Science–Methodology–Juvenile literature. |
    Research–Methodology–Juvenile literature.
Classification: LCC Q175.2 .G43 2024 | DDC 507.2/1–dc23/eng/20230816
LC record available at https://lccn.loc.gov/2023035059

Printed in the United States of America

Amanda Gebhardt is a curriculum writer and editor and a life-long learner. She lives in Ann Arbor, Michigan, with her husband, two kids, and one playful pup named Cookie.